D1092587

Valiant Imperial
Warriors
2200 Years Ago

图书在版编目(CIP)数据

2200 年前的帝国雄兵:英文/吴晓丛,郭佑民主编.—西安:
世界图书出版西安公司,2007.10(2016.10 重印)

ISBN 978-7-5062-8996-2

Ⅰ.2... Ⅱ.①吴...②郭... Ⅲ.秦始皇陵—兵马俑—图集
Ⅳ.K878.92

中国版本图书馆 CIP 数据核字(2007)第 151250 号

Valiant Imperial Warriors 2200 Years Ago

Chief editor:Wu Xiaocong   Guo Youmin
Written by:Wu Xiaocong
Photographer:Guo Youmin   Xia Juxian   Guo Yan
Translated by:Wen Tao   Wu Guojun
Editor:Fan Xin

Publisher:Xi'an World Publishing Corporation
Address:85 Beidajie, Xi'an,China
ISBN 978-7-5062-8996-2
Price:150.00(英)

2016.10

Valiant Imperial Warriors 2200 Years Ago

Contents

Preface

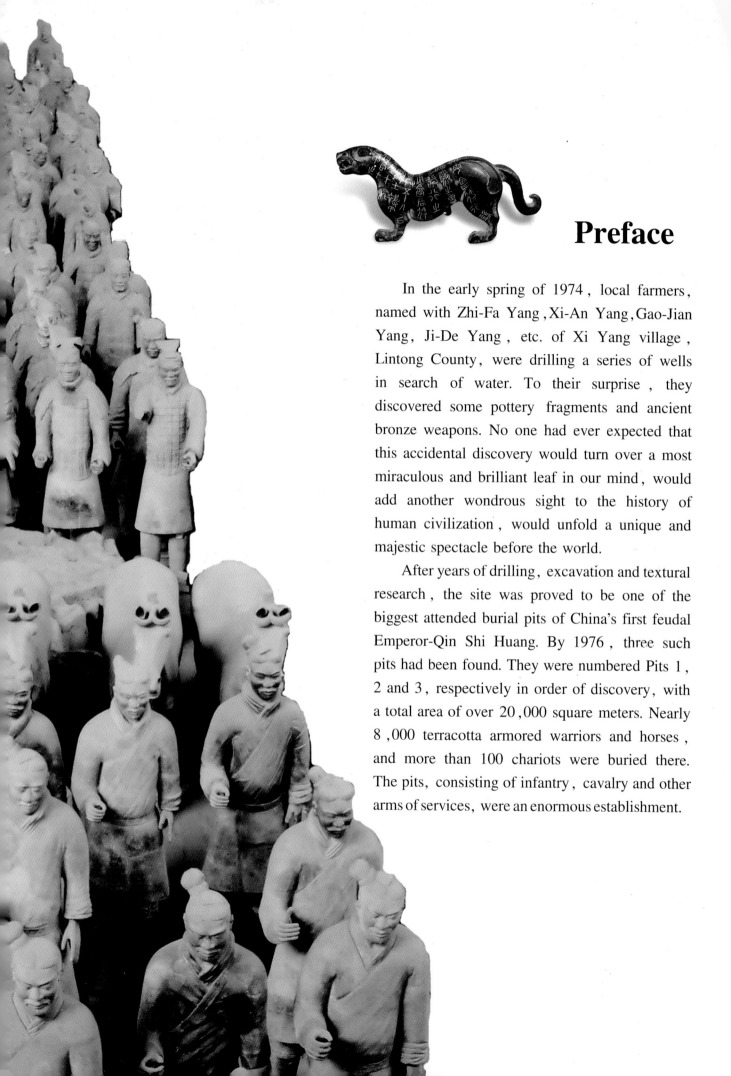

Preface

In the early spring of 1974, local farmers, named with Zhi-Fa Yang, Xi-An Yang, Gao-Jian Yang, Ji-De Yang, etc. of Xi Yang village, Lintong County, were drilling a series of wells in search of water. To their surprise, they discovered some pottery fragments and ancient bronze weapons. No one had ever expected that this accidental discovery would turn over a most miraculous and brilliant leaf in our mind, would add another wondrous sight to the history of human civilization, would unfold a unique and majestic spectacle before the world.

After years of drilling, excavation and textural research, the site was proved to be one of the biggest attended burial pits of China's first feudal Emperor-Qin Shi Huang. By 1976, three such pits had been found. They were numbered Pits 1, 2 and 3, respectively in order of discovery, with a total area of over 20,000 square meters. Nearly 8,000 terracotta armored warriors and horses, and more than 100 chariots were buried there. The pits, consisting of infantry, cavalry and other arms of services, were an enormous establishment.

The discovery of Emperor Qin's terracotta army is world-shaking. From then on, the discoveries have been persistent for almost thirty years. In 1979, a museum was founded upon the sites. It turned into not only a famous scenic area but also a modern on-site museum in China. Now, the pits 1, 2, 3 and a multiple exhibition building are open. In the last twenty years, 50 million visitors, including over 100 heads of different countries, have visited the museum. Mr. Guang-yao Li, the former Prime Minister of Singapore, praised it as the 'miracle of the world, pride of the Nation'. In 1978, Jacques Chirac, the President of France said that is was the Eighth Wonder of the world, which has wildly spread and become synonym of the Terracotta Army museum. What's more, it was exhibited in about 30 countries all over the world with 10,000 visitors being astounded.

In 1987, the Emperor Qin's mausoleum, including Emperor Qin's Terracotta Army museum, was placed on UNESCO's list as a world-class culture heritage site, which leads to more and more people paying attention to the mausoleum. At the same time, the archaeologists ceaselessly acquired great productions from the mausoleum. Recently, a building-project about Qin Shi Huang's mausoleum on-site garden was started. This garden will display the rich cultural relics of Qin's mausoleum on a large scale.

With the discovery of Qin's mausoleum, the resplendence of an old dynasty, which had exited before 2,200 years, becomes more and more clear.

The Service Centre

The external view of Pit 3

The external view of Pit 1

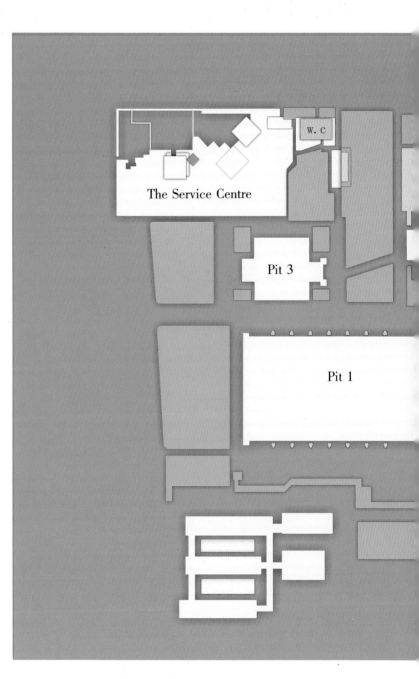

The Service Centre

W. C

Pit 3

Pit 1

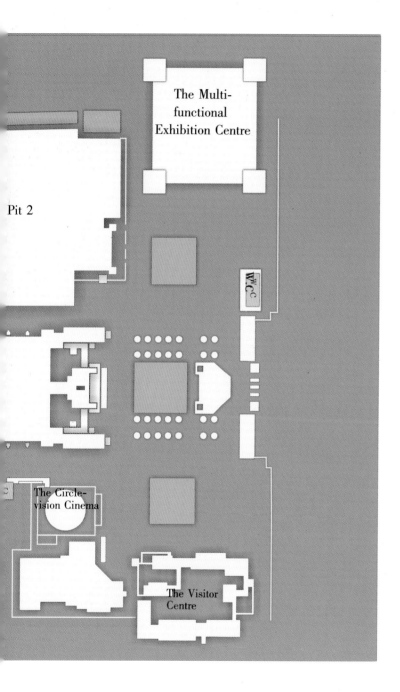

The Multi-
functional
Exhibition Centre

Pit 2

W.C.C

The Circle-
vision Cinema

The Visitor
Centre

The external view of the
Multi-functional Exhibition Centre

The external view of Pit 2

The Circle-vision Cinema

The Battle Formation of Emperor Qin's Terracotta Warriors and Horses

Emperor Qin Shi Huang
— The First Emperor in Chinese History

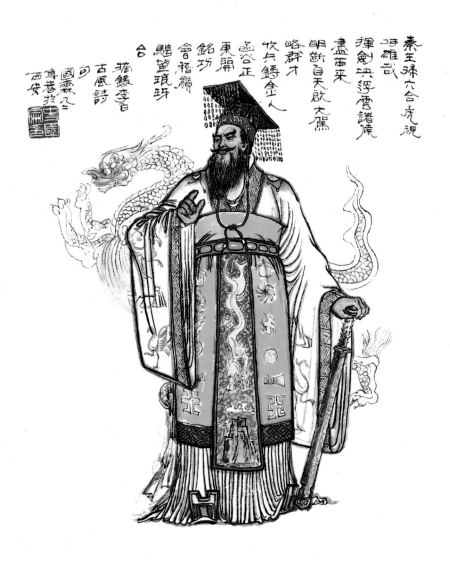

The Portrait of Emperor Qin Shi Huang

To realize Emperor Qin's Terracotta Army, we have to know Emperor Qin Shi Huang first.

Qin Shi Huang, whose family name was Ying and first name was Zheng, was born in 259 BC and died in 210 BC. He was the first organizer of the Nationally centralized feudal empire and a great talent and bold vision. The times he lived in were in turmoil of war, bloody murder and in wrack and ruin. And Emperor Qin was really a giant full of romance and spirituality.

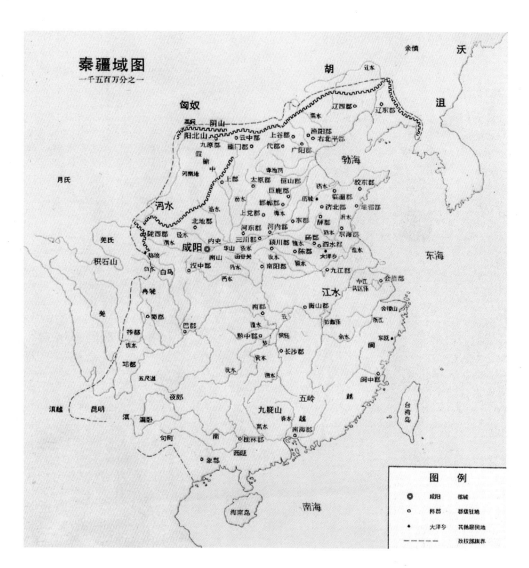

Emperor Qin's territory

In the later times of the Warring Periods, the whole of China was divided into many vassal countries such as Qi, Chu, Yan, Han, Zhao, Wei and Qi. In order to defend territories and strengthen national power, some policies, such as developing agriculture, strengthening military affairs, were taken. Wars among those seven countries were becoming very drastic and lasted from months to years. For example, in the famous war in Chang Ping, Zhao was forced to surrender to Qin because of the lack of food, the debris of which could be still seen in the site of Gao Ping, Shanxi Province.

Bronze bell

The lasting war and intersected situation had an terrible impact not only on dumb millions but also on productivity. The disunity in handwriting and money counteracted the development of merchandise trading and culture amalgamation. The coterminous two countries set different kinds of tollgates to destroy each other. In this situation, the catastrophic destruction couldn't have existed any longer. Furthermore, to realise unification and to bury the hatchet was an inevitable demand of the historical development.

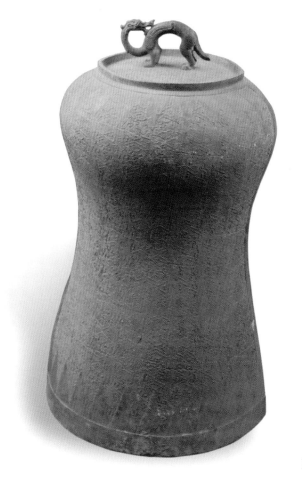

Bronze drum

At that time, Qin was a puny country and was looked down on by other six countries. In 356 BC, Shang Yang's political reform was pushed, which cores were to manage state affairs legally, to encourage plantation and join battle, to allow domainial bargaining and to possess privately possession and so on. It was really a profound revolution in the fields of politics, economy

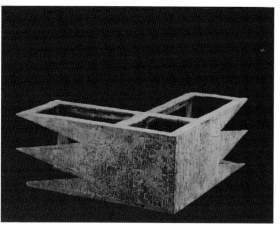

Bronze joint (architecture)

Iron sword with gold handle

and ideology. Although ShangYang was put into death finally, the Qin Dynasty developed rapidly. In the later 100 years, its national power was greatly increased. Up to the times of King Zhao, Qin turned into a wealthy country with millions of fighters, chariots and horses. Obviously, only Qin could unify the whole country.

Emperor Qin Shi Huang was born in 259 BC, according to history. One was really needed to uniform the intersected countries and eradicate dissident. In the Warring Period, continual battle helped to bring up Ying Zheng's go-getting character.

Emperor Qin's life was full of romance. His father, Yi (later called Zi Chu), was the grandson of King Zhao and the son of King Xiao Wen. Yi was not regarded highly because his obscurity and was sent to country Zhao as a hostage. His life was out at the elbows and out of order.

All was changed dramatically with the appearance of Lü Buwei, who was a businessman in Yang Zhai. He possessed not only the sensitivity to pursue commercial profit, but also political and strategic mind. He recognized Yi while dealing with business in Han Dan city. He believed that, by making use of Yi's special status, a political gamble could be done without any expense.

Bronze pot depicting people playing the game Sheyan

Helping Yi ascend the kingdom was Lü Buwei's immediate political goal. He exerted a series of artful strategy. Firstly, he presented 2.5 kilograms gold to Yi, which could consort him with a lot of friends. Then he came to Zhao and bribed Queen HuaYang, who was the imperial concubine of King Xiaowen. In this way, Yi was able to be back to King Qin and confirmed as prince of King Qin. A year later, King Xiaowen was dead and Yi, who was called King Zhuangxiang, ascended the kingdom successfully.

In fact, there existed a secret, which finally brought on a political crisis, between Yi and Lü Bu Wei. As a hostage in King Zhao, Yi met Zhao Ji, L? Bu Wei's concubine, and in time fell in

The Tiger Token of the East County

love with her. The scandal irritated Lü Buwei deeply. In order to realize his political goal, Lü Buwei persuaded himself to send Zhaoji to Yi as his wife. After they got married, a boy was born in January and was called Ying Zheng. According to historical records, Zhao Ji disguised the fact that she lived together with Lü Buwei and was already pregnant, so no one could really know who was Ying Zheng's father. Thus Emperor Qin was regarded as the bastard of Lü Buwei, and he was also called Lü Zheng. Historian considered that it was fictitious. It was just a falsity designed by Lü Buwei.

Of course, whether Emperor was a bastard played no role in his later historical contribution. From descriptive records, Emperor Qin was an all-powerful and meritorious man with big eyes, nice nose and strapping stature.

In the 247 BC, Qin's father (King Zhuang Xiang) died because of his poor health. Ying Zheng, who was only 13 years old, inherited his father's regality. He was too young to reign this complicated political position, what he could do was only to depend on the Queen Mother and ministers. In this way, Lü Buwei and the Queen Mother dominated the whole empire without any problems.

As is described above, Emperor Qin's Queen Mother Zhao had a special relationship with Lü Buwei. After King Zhuang Xiang's death and Emperor Qin's succession, she felt quite lonely and restarted an affair with Lü Buwei. Lü Buwei, with the feeling of being aware of possible ruin, being afraid of Emperor Qin's chastisement, found a chaperone, whose name was Lao Ai, to accompany the Queen Mother Zhao so as to cast off this perplexing relationship. With the help of the Queen Mother Zhao, Lao Ai possessed great power and plenty of money, even he alleged that he was Ying Zheng's stepfather. Without question, all of these scandals badly hurt Ying Zheng. But silently bore his suffering, and waited for his opportunity to have revenge for himself.

In 238 BC, when Ying Zheng was 22 years old, he went through his coronation in Ji Nian Palace according to his Empire's system and began to govern his empire himself. Eliminating disaster, carrying out political reforms and strengthening the Nation's might, he finally realized his dream to unify the whole state. At that time, Qin finished a wonderful preparation for annihilating the other six rival states. In military affairs, he kept expanding military strength and putting the army under rigorous training. In diplomacy, he kept the policy of segregation and even spent lots of money on sabotaging the ministers in the other six rival states,

The Tiger Token
of Du (district)

Iron halberd

which created certain confusion. All this helped him to sweep away one after another his six rival states. He was successful in his policy of selecting wise men. He appointed some intellectuals in areas that were not Qin's subject, such as Li Si, Wei Liao, Yao Jia, and these wisemen played a great role on the business of unifying country.

In 236 BC, Emperor Qin began the task of conquering the six other states that existed at that time in ancient China, the states of Qi, Chu, Yan, Han, Zhao and Wei. All the territory of those six rival states was won by Qin's Army. In the ten years, the army of Qin showed great capability to kill enemies and reoccupy the dominions.

In 221 BC, Emperor Qin put an end to the chaos of several hundreds of years after the Spring and Autumn Period. Followed by attacking Bei Yue (lies in Zhe Jiang Province, Fu Jian Province and so on) and assaulting with Hun, Emperor Qin consolidated the border area and

A starter tile with toad pattern

established the Qin Dynasty-the first unified feudal state in China's history. The Qin Dynasty, focusing in Xian Yang, was an expansive nation large in area. Its territory extended from the sea in the south and east, Gan Qing in the west and Mount Yin and the area of Liao Dong in the north. The Qin Dynasty was not only a powerful nation at that time, but also in its core politics, economy and civilization. Emperor Qin knew it was important for him to establish and solidify his authority so as to govern the nation effectively.

Before his unification, the highest gover-

nor was called King. Because of his greatest contribution to the practice of government, Qin ordered his ministers to provide him a proper title. The suggestion was "Tai Huang" but Qin considered himself higher, so he decided to call himself "The Beginning Emperor", which meant that his achievements could be handed down forever. Evermore, the appellation "Emperor" was used for thousands of years. To show the difference with others, Emperor Qin instituted a series of new policies. For example, the order of Emperor was called "Zhi" and "Zhao" and his great seal could only be called "Xi". Another example, "Zheng" could only be used by the Emperor called himself. What's more, adopting the theory in the Spring and Autumn Period, Emperor Qin made the regulation that only black

Bronze plate with scripture

could be regarded as a noblest symbol. Although seeming to be superstitious today, but at that time, they undoubtedly met the needs of intensifying imperial power.

Of course, the above policies were limited in form. To strengthen his imperial power, the fateful innovation Emperor Qin did was to establish a series of rigorous feudalization ranged from centrality to region. Probably his greatest contribution to the practice of government in China was the establishment of the centralized States. He established Three Gong and Nine Qing in the centre. In this way, Emperor Qin kept himself the head of military affairs and thus avoided being neglected.

Emperor Qin abolished the feudal system and thus divided the country into 36 prefectures (and later increased to 46 prefectures) that were further broken down into counties, townships, Tings and Lis. He appointed twelve ministers who helped him make decisions on State affairs. Once all these acts were taken, they played a crucial role not only in governing the whole dynasty at that time but also in laying the foundation of 2000 years of feudalization in China.

Qin Shi Huang showed a great interest on construction which showed his capability. Early before he realized his unification, he had already built many gorgeous palaces in Xia Yang, Yong Cheng etc. After unification, he believed that nothing could display his achievements except building a palace. He undertook a vast construction program within the Empire, expanded the size of his tomb and had large numbers of palaces built. Over 270 palaces were discovered around his capital-XianYang. In the last ten years, palace sites about pit 1, 2 and 3 were found. Archaeologists detected that the palace was a hath pace construction, its different palaces were connected by gallant pavilions. It was really a pity that it was burnt down at the end of Qin Dynasty. What we could see today is only a relic.

Today, we sing high praise for Emperor Qin's establishment on feudalization, but the uniform measures Emperor Qin had taken in eliminating differences amongst differing areas, in expediting the development of the economy and civilization were worked on enormously. The uniform measures include:

Firstly, Qin standardized the system of coinage. In the Warring Period, coins used were quite disordered not only in weight but also in shape, which really brought difficulty when merchandising currency. In 221 BC, Emperor Qin ordered to abolish each country's coin and enforced a new currency system. The shape of this kind of new coin was circular, its centre being a hollow square. Henceforth, it was used until the later Qing Dynasty.

Secondly, the system of weights and measurements were sta ndardized. To realise the unification of the whole nation's weights and measurements, Emperor Qin ordered that regulation in Shang Yang's reformation could be only used. And the related inscription was imprinted in official regulators. In this century, those regulators were found in Shan Dong Province, Shaan Xi Province, Jiang Su Province and so on. According to the records, long measure in Qin Dynasty was inch, chi, zhang and yin. 10 inches came up to 1 chi, 10 chi to 1 zhang and 10 zhang to 1 yin. 1 chi amounts to 23.1 centimeters. At that time, weight measure was he, sheng, dou and hu and its scale measure was zhu, liang, jin, jun and shi.

Thirdly, Emperor Qin unified the standardization of handwriting. Because of the long-term abruptions in the later Warring Period, there existed prodigious differences in different areas, which counteracted the development of the economy and culture, not to mention the advancement of politics. In this situation, Li Si was ordered to establish 'Small Seal Script' and generalized it to the whole dynasty. In the view of our expert, compared with other six rival states, Qin's new handwriting was a successful reformation not only in its orderly shape, but also because it's easy to write. Undoubtedly, it was a wonderful change in the history of handwriting development.

Last but not least, Emperor Qin ordered that the width of carriage axles should be exactly six feet. In the 220 BC, the road around Xian Yang was built. In the later eight years, so as to

Bronze scales

Bronze Measuring Bowl

defend from intrusion from the Hun, the road from Xian Yang to Jiu Yuan County (today's Nei Meng) was construct, which was over 700 kilometers. These roads helped to keep the relation with areas far away from XianYang and played an important role on consolidating the regime.

Except for the above unification measures, Emperor Qin regulated the nation's legal system according to King Qin's original law. To keep out invaders, he ordered to rebuild and connect the defensive walls of the states. After ten years' hard work, The Great Wall, which was over 10,000 miles long, was finally connected from Liao Dong (today's Liao Yang, in Liao Ning Province) to Lin Yao (today's Min county, in Gansu Province). From then on, The Great Wall, created to great astonishment, lies in the north of China. It is a monument full of creativity.

As an outstanding feudal monarch, Emperor Qin showed a certain courage and insight and was even called "the only Emperor in thousands of years". But, he was an infrequent and dictatorial despot. It was just his autocratic dominion that led to the quick death of Qin Dynasty. Along with the stability of his imperial power, Emperor Qin became more and more avaricious. According to historical records and archaeological discovery, law in Qin Dynasty became very cruel. For example, there were almost ten kinds of execution, which reflected a kind of slavery. Emperor Qin read reports from all parts of the country in order to be aware of problems everywhere in his domain. He had the reports weighed (writings were inscribed on bamboo or

Bronze standard weight
in Qin Dynasty

wood at that time) and would not rest until he had read a certain weight of reports. It could be seen that the so-called law to protect the whole country was in fact a tool that met Emperor Qin's private needs.

Confucian scholars were murdered, persecuting large numbers of scholars and thus destroyed Chinese culture, having an enormous influence among all that Qin did.

The destruction of many ancient records and Confucian writings happened in 213 BC. One day, Chun Yu Yue, one of King Zhao's scholars was not satisfied with some ministers' greasiness and confirmed that not only the system of county but the feudal system should be

The Great Wall

taken in Qin Dynasty. As we know, Emperor Qin abolished the feudal system as soon as he began his reformation. What Chun Yu Yue said was not a bit suitable although he was cordial. One minister, named Li Si, pointed out that the scholars attacked the Emperor and system, which could finally endanger imperial power. It was all because of books and records scholars read. Consequently, the destruction of many ancient records and Confucian writings had been carried through.

We can clearly know that what Li Si said was preposterous from a logistic viewpoint, but it rightly met the needs of Emperor Qin on unifying the whole nation by being obscurant. And then, it turned into reality. According to Li Si's suggestion, all the historical records, except Qin Ji, a curatorial book and plating book, were incinerated. Furthermore, freedom of speech was banned. Only 30 days were given to burn books, otherwise chastisement would be taken. By this way, conventional Chinese culture met a terrible catastrophe.

In the later year, another sanguinary event Emperor Qin made was called "burying the Confucian scholars alive". It was said that twice Confucian scholars were buried, one was in Xian Yang where over 460 scholars were burned and another was in Lin Tong, about 700 were burned. Today, we can still find the "Vale of Confucian scholars" which beyond all doubt, brought us great sorrow.

The Valley of the "Murdered Confucian scholars"

The goal of burying books and burying Confucian scholars alive was to consolidate feudal regime, but all things went contrary to Emperor Qin's wishes. Just as we know, those who vanquished the Qin Dynasty, such as Liu Bang and

The tomb of the Second Qin Emperor

Xiang Yu, were not Confusion scholars at all. Emperor Qin was so despicable a despot that all those who backed an opposite proposal were punished. In 210 BC, in his fifth tour of inspection, Emperor Qin died.

In fact, Emperor Qin's death meant that an extremely arrogant dynasty would be ended. It was rightly his truculence that caused different kinds of social disharmony to be on the verge of breaking out. Hu Hai became the second Emperor that year. He was not an able politician and was unable to make decisions. Hu Hai also lived an even more luxurious life than his father. In 209 BC, a peasant rebellion led by Chen Sheng and Wu Guang happened in Da Ze village (today's County Su, in An Hui Province) and swept over the country. In 206 BC, a group of insurrectionists reached Xian Yang and seized hold of Zi Ying. The Qin Dynasty, a feudal state once so lively and unchallengeable, became the shortest-lived feudal dynasty which lasted only 15 years. Despite its short duration, it was a great influence and laid the foundation for the success of future dynasties.

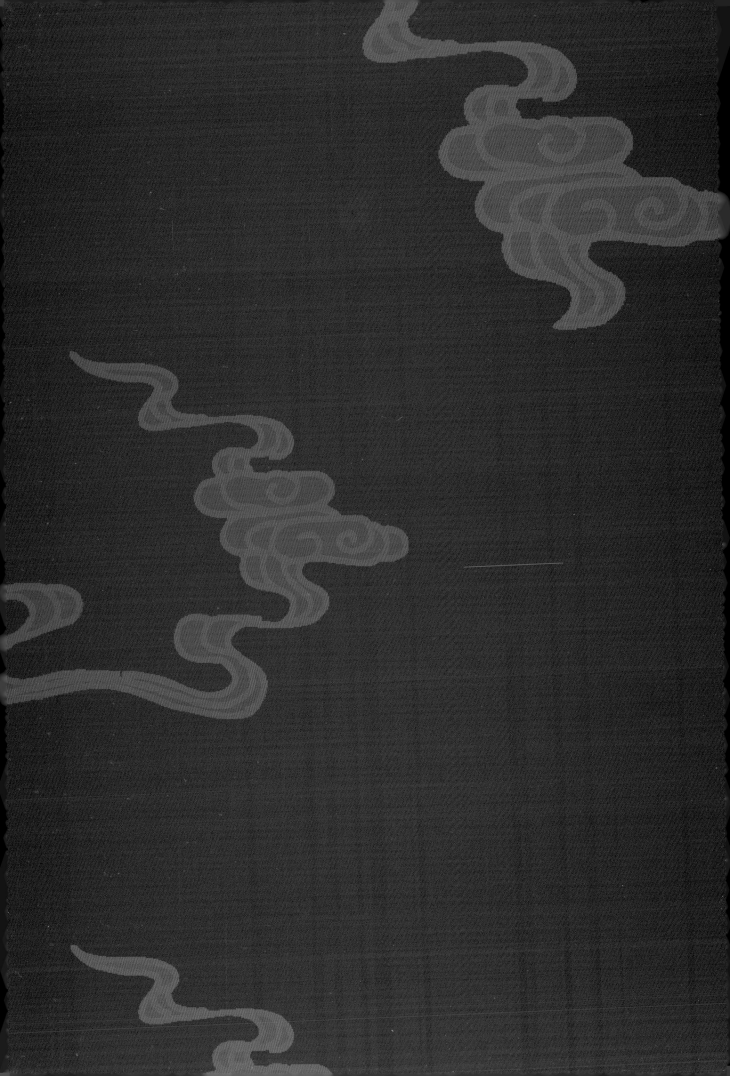

Emperor Qin's Terracotta Museum
— The Biggest On-Site Museum in China

Emperor Qin's mausoleum, situated at the northern foot of Mount Li, some 35 kilometers east of Xi'an city, is one of the biggest on-site museums in China.

In China's history, almost all emperors placed great importance on constructing mausoleums because of their viewpoints about the undiminished soul. Emperors tried their best to construct mausoleums; it was the same with Emperor Qin. According to the records, on his thirteenth birthday, Emperor Qin began to construct mausoleums for himself upon the foot of Mount Li. It soon became one of Qin's most involved affairs. Construction took 38 years from 247 BC to 208 BC and divided into three stages, having as many as 720,000 conscripts. Si Ma Qian, a historian in Han Dynasty, wrote as follows: "they dug through three streams and poured molten copper for

The Mausoleum
of Emperor Qin

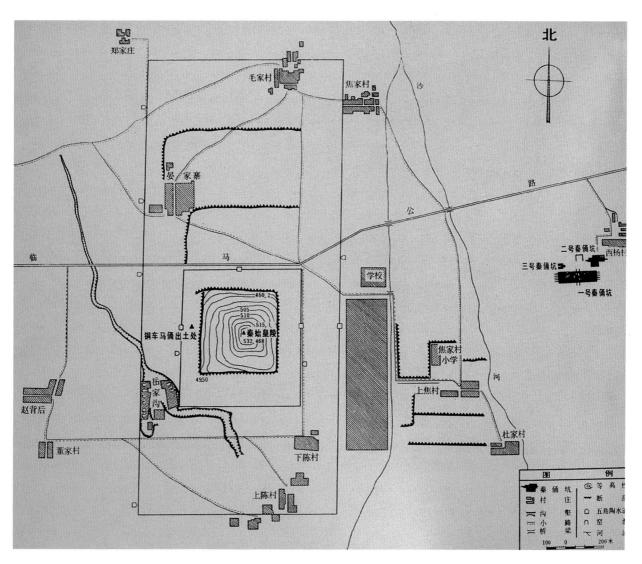

Map of Emperor Qin's Mausoleum

the outer coffin, and the tomb was fitted with models of palaces, pavilions and officials, as well as fine vessels, precious stones and other rarities". Its safety precautions were so thorough that once it was infringed, the apparatus would run automatically. The coffin was decorated luxuriously. All the ladies who had no children were ordered to follow the Emperor to the grave. All the tomb builders were also buried alive in order to keep the tomb secret." The analogous records could be seen in Han Shu, another text by Ban Gu. The description tells us that Emperor Qin Shi Huang's mausoleum was actually an underground kingdom of grandiose structure and a magnificent treasure.

The preliminary data obtained through archaeological excavation and drilling reveal that the

Bronze musical bell

burial mound, which was a solid triangular shape, was 115 meters high 2200 years ago. Due to the passage of time it is reduced to 76 meters today. The burial mound was 345 meters from east to west and 350 meters from north to south, around which were constructions such as rampart, palaces and so on. The underground sepulcher was more abundance. There were 30 meters to the center of the tomb, which was used to lay the Emperor's casket. With the Emperor's tomb as

Phoenix designed starter tile

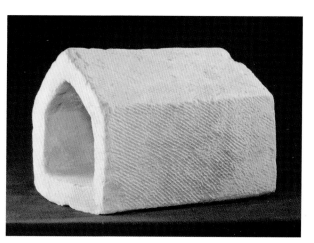

Pentagon-shaped water pipe

the center, some 100 satellite pits and tombs have been found within the area of 56.25 square kilometers and more continues to be discovered. In those satellite pits and tombs, pits of bronze chariots and horses, pits of rare birds and animals, pits of pottery acrobats, pits of civil officials and pits of stone armor and helmets can be seen. In recent years, there were millions of relics to be discovered, including lots of unique treasures. All discoveries play a great role for us to realise its construction, to explore the secret of this mausoleum. The details are as follows:

Kneeling pottery figures

Terracotta civil
officials

Terracotta civil officials

The pits of the civil officials

In the year 2000, this new burial pit located southwest of the emperor's tomb mound was discovered. It was over 140 square meters, in which 12 figures were found. The hands held no weapons, but were crossed at the waist and covered by long, loose sleeves. Furthermore, vehicles made in wood and bones of living horses were found. It is estimated that these pottery figures might be the mid-ranking civil officials who served in the Central Government of the Qin Empire.

Amour suit made of stone

Stone helmets

The pits of stone armor and helmets

In 1998, a large burial pit containing stone armor and stone helmets was discovered. It was some 200 meters southeast of the emperor's mausoleum. The pit is rectangular in shape, covering an area of over 13,000 square meters. Nearly 80 stone armor suits and 40 stone helmets have been unearthed. These objects were scattered in disarray on the bottom of the pit. Several pillars supported a wooden ceiling coated by layers of straw. Different sections of the pit were separated by rammed earth. Judging from the features, archaeologists divide the armor suits into three categories: small stone flakes, medium stone flakes and large stone flakes. Small stone flakes are thin but exquisitely made, just like fish scales. The armor suits are composed of over 800 stone flakes. Medium stone flakes make up most of the stone armors that have been discovered. Most of the stone flakes are rectangular or square with tiny holes for linking them or for decoration. Only one piece of large stone flake has been unearthed. All the armor suits were made the same size as real armor coats and helmets. According to the archaeologists, they were not for practical use like the iron or leather armor of that area. These might have been specially made as funeral objects for Emperor Qin Shi Huang.

The pits of the pottery acrobats

In 1999, archaeologists found another pit within the area of 800 square meters in the south of the stone armor and helmets pit. The trial excavation unearthed 11 pottery figurines. Similar to real people in size, the figurines were only clothed with shorts in a shape similar to those of woman's miniskirt today. Some appear tall and strong while some others short and slim. Exquisitely made, the figures vary in posture. One has his hand raised and another holds a piece of his outfit. Compared with the serious expressions on the terracotta warriors, these figures were more active and expressive. According to an analysis of the restored figures, archaeologists said, different from the terracotta warriors, these pottery figures might be the acrobats who served in the Emperor Qin's imperial palace, portraying the splendid acrobatic act of the Qin Dynasty.

Terracotta acrobats

Terracotta acrobats

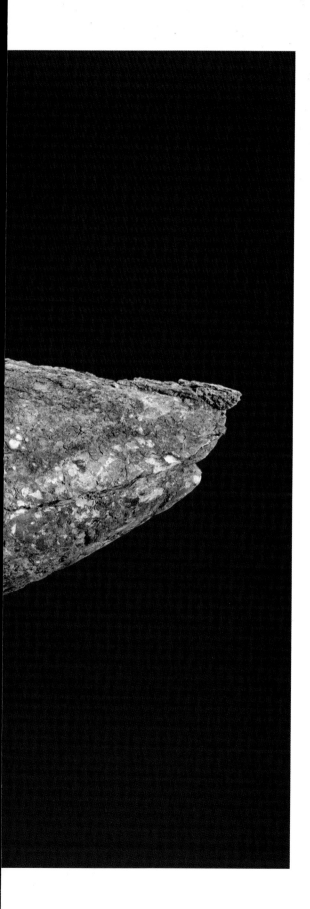

The pits of the bronze water birds

In the year 2000, thirty-one bronze water birds had been unearthed within the confines of the wall on the northeast side of the mausoleum, with an area of about 1,000 square meters. The size of these bronze water birds is the same as the real animal. They were placed in a setting full of water. About 31 birds, such as swans, geese and wild goose, were unearthed. What's more, several pottery figures were unearthed in this pit. These pottery figures show different expressions. What on earth this pit was designed for is still an enigma.

Bronze mallard

Bronze crane

The Discovery and Excavation of
Qin's Terracotta Army

These pits of pottery figures are 1.5 kilometers east of Emperor Qin's mausoleum and it is the largest and most stirring of the burial pits. The grand scene of the mustering of an army, going out for a battle not only lays out a powerful imperial army, but also offers us information to study the ancient Chinese battle formations, weaponry, strategies and tactical thinking.

Pit No.1

Pit 1, the largest pit, is rectangular in shape. It measures 230 meters long from east to west, 62 meters wide from north to south, covering an area of 14,260 square meters. The pit is estimated to contain over 6,000 terracotta armoured warriors and horses, with over 40 woody

Infantry and chariots in Pit 1

◀ Vanguard of the Army in formation in Pit 1

Back view of the army formation in Pit 1

chariots. These infantries and chariots form quadrate battalions. In the front of the pit there are three rows of vanguards, 68 in each, totaling 204 soldiers who were originally equipped with genuine bows and crossbows. They constitute the vanguard. Behind the galley, rammed partition walls dividing Pit 1 into 11 latitudinal passage-way where stand facing east 38 columns of warriors with horse-drawn chariots deployed in a regular pattern. Most of the warriors are armour-clad, holding such weapons as spears, barbed spears, halberds or crossbows. As heavily-armed warriors, they make up the main body of the army Pit. 1 Around the outer edge, there is one row of soldiers with crossbows facing south, north and west respectively as the flanks to guard the sides and rear of the army. The formation is well-organized.

Remains of a chariot and terracotta charioteer ▶

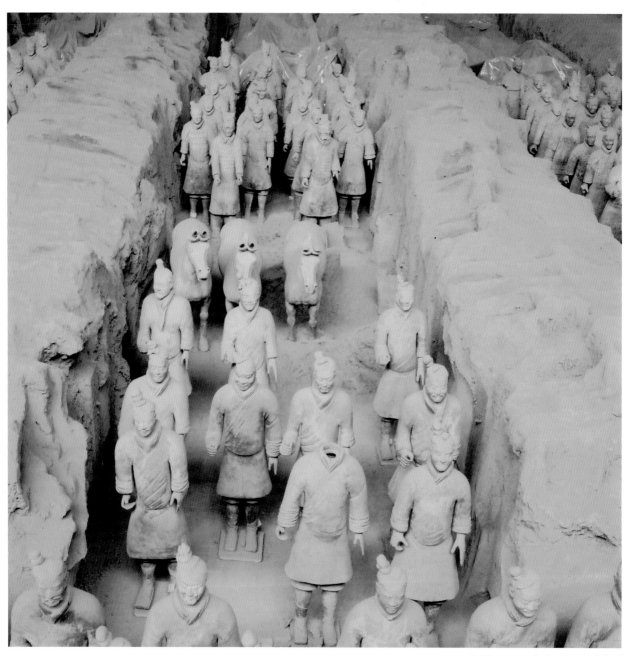

Infantry and chariot in Pits 1

Back view of the army formation in Pit 1 ▶

Flank of the army formation in Pit 1

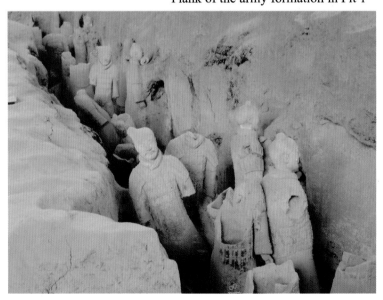

Flank of the army formation in Pit 1

Partition of the army formation in Pit 1

Terracotta Charioteer and infantry

Terracotta chariot and horses

Remains of chariot and horses

Pit No.2

Located 20 meters to the north of Pit1 at the eastern end, Pit 2, is a "L" shape with a protruding rectangular area at the northern corner. The pit is 124 meters long and 98 meters wide, with coverage of nearly 6,000 square meters. By drilling and testing for excavation at a few points, it contains over 900 terracotta warriors and 350 terracotta horses together with about

Terracotta Warriors and Horses
of Emperor Qin Shi Huang

Cavalry and horses excavated in Pit 2

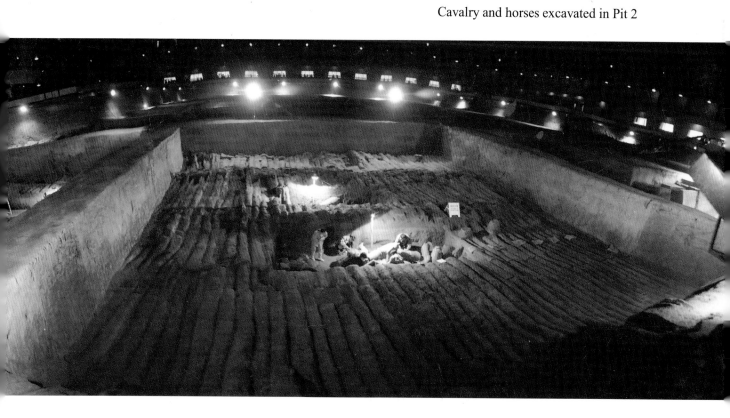

Excavation site of Pit 2

A terracotta general

Kneeling archer in Pit 2

90 wooden chariots in a battle formation of a mixed army of infantry, cavalry and chariots. The formation is made up of four small arrays. The first, situated in the front of the L-shaped battle formation, is an array of 330 standing archers in armour, all holding crossbows. The standing arches are placed on the outer flanks whereas the kneeling ones are in the center. In real combats, the two kinds of arches alternate their postures and shoot by turns with arrows showering upon attackers. To the right of the L-shape is the second array composed of 64 chariots, each of which carries three warriors. The third array consisting of chariots, infantry and cavalry is a column formation in the middle of the L-shape army. This array, with 19 chariots as the main force aided by a small number of infantrymen and cavalrymen, is a mobile supplement. To the left of the L-shape formation is the fourth and last array made up mainly of 108 odd cavalrymen on saddled horses in a rectangular pattern. Pit 2 consists of smaller arrays and camps enclosed by bigger ones, which are interrelated and in symmetrical shape. The mixed formation of charioteers, infantry and cavalry were in particular an important development and change in army's formation. This shows the innovative military strategy of the Qin army to grasp the initiative in war.

Painted kneeling archer in Pit 2

Pit No.3

Pit 3 is located 20 meters to the north of Pit 1 at the western end and 120 meters to the east of Pit 2. It is of U-shape, with the area less than 500 square meters. Only 66 pottery figures and one chariot drawn by four horses were unearthed in this pit. At the eastern end of the pit, there is a slope acting as point of entry, followed by an ornate canopied chariot with four armored soldiers. Although Pit 3 is the smallest of the three pits, it plays a more incontestable role compared with Pit 1 and Pit 2. The warriors are not arranged in a battle formation, but stand opposite to each other in two rows in the formation of the guard of honor. They hold bamboo weapons with pointed heads for self-defense. Unearthed also in this pit were deer horns and animal bones found in the north chamber. Pit 3 is now known as the command center of the entire army.

The dissimilar meaning of each pit and the relationship between the three pits indicate that the whole attendant burial pits were skillfully designed. It contains not only the headquarters, which is heavily guarded, but also the ever-victorious powerful army. Being up against such a gigantic scene helps us to imagine Emperor Qin's great achievement and grand ancient battlefield.

Overview of Pit 3

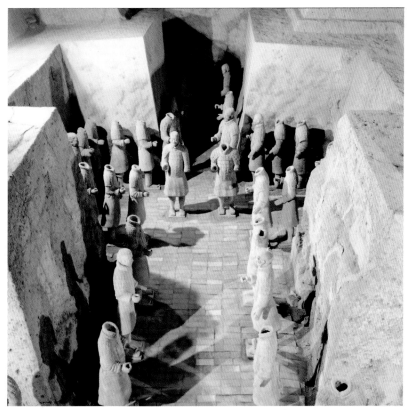

Southern Chamber in Pit 3

Part of Pit 3

Amoured guards in Pit 3

Northern Chamber in Pit 3

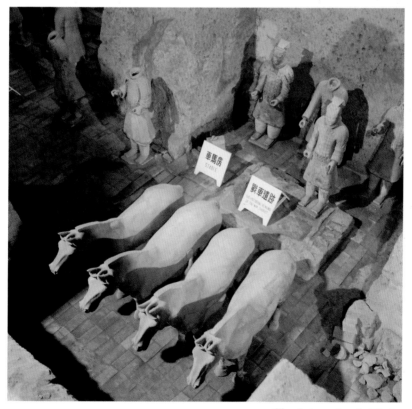

Chariot section in Pit 3

Part of Pit 3

Excavating site

Previous excavation works

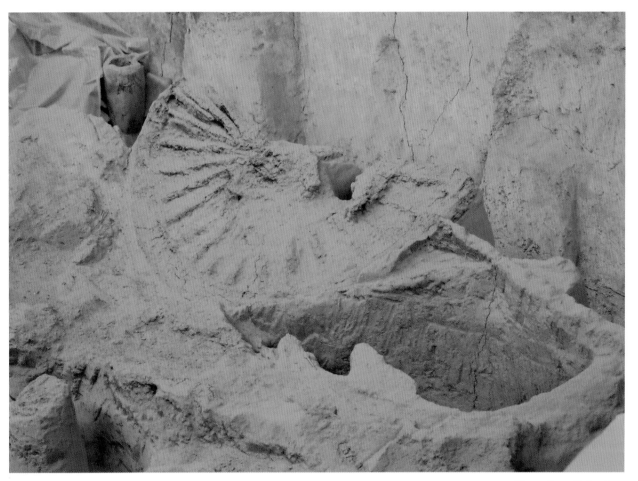

Remains of chariots

Today, when we excitedly visit these life-like terracotta figures and powerful lineup, those archeologist and restorers who are conscientious to man's cultural heritage can change ruin into a wonder that moves us very much.

The total area of these three pits is over 20,000 square meters. Ever since the terracotta warriors and horses were discovered in 1974, only 1/3 of the 32 restoration works are finished although discoveries continue and restoration work is persistent. Mending broken figures becomes a painstaking work for archeological workers. For many years, Emperor Qin's

Previous restoration site

Part of the army formation

Terracotta Army Museum has been not only a grandiose martial museum of ancient china but also an archaeological and relic restoration site, which has been paid great attention to by world historians and archaeologists.

According to the records of historians, Emperor Qin's mausoleum was prodigiously damaged. Although abundant data was not found about who damaged the mausoleum, it can be proved that most of the ground construction and terracotta pits were intentionally damaged. Some relational experts consider that it is likely that Xiang Yu, a rebel in the Qin Dynasty, burnt Emperor Qin's palace and his mausoleum in 206 BC. These three pits were built from earth and wood. When putting things in order, people found that fire damaged the construction of the pits and that the collapsed roof broke the terracotta warrior into fragments.

A lot of hard work has been done with the aim of protecting this valuable treasure of the world and resurrection of the gigantic army of the Qin Dynasty. According to the rules of archaeology, the three pits should be excavated scientifically. The archaeologists have to unearth

Part of the army formation

the items, take pictures and record data diligently so it is obtained, explainable and thus rejuvenate more information to become available. At the same time, the experts who restore cultural relics and scientifically protect them entered the pits and developed their research. Because none of warriors and horses were whole when they were unearthed, some of them were in thousands of pieces, mending these broken figures can really be an arduous task for archaeologists and other workers. As soon as the warriors and horses were unearthed, the experts numbered each of them. Each fragment has been marked to indicate where the item was found and to which statue it might belong. In order to prevent the paint from flaking and fading after being brought to the surface, researchers in the museum have worked with foreign experts for many years. After years of research, several new technological methods were invented. Furthermore, multimedia is used in the museum in collecting and displaying the correlative data. What the museum did raised systematic archaeological information with integrity, allowing scientific skills reach a higher level and accumulated more experience to the excavation and scientific management of Emperor Qin's Terracotta Army Museum.

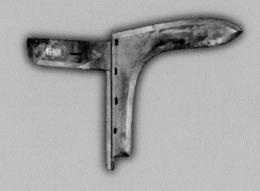

The Unique Bronze Weapons in the Terracotta Pits

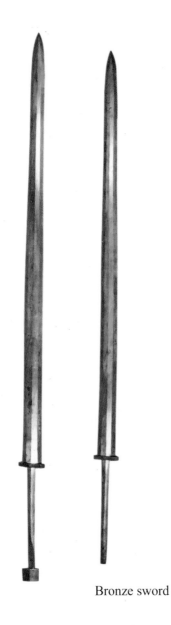

Bronze spear

Although the warriors were made of pottery, the weapons in their hands were of the bronze in real battles so as to make the powerful line-up realistic. The weapons can be divided into three categories: long weapons, short weapons and long-range weapons, such as spears, halberds, the Shu, the Pi, swords, Wu hooks and crossbows and so on. Especially the Pi and Wu hook are the first of their kind so far to be unearthed. Approximately tens of thousands of weapons have been unearthed from the partly excavated pits. Inscriptions of Xiao Zhuan, which was very exiguous, could be found on most of the weapons. Some described the time in which the weapons were made; some bore the name of official unit for manufacturing arms. All these weapons are

Bronze sword

Bronze arrowheads

quite significant not only in studying the level of craftsmanship but also to accurately judge the time the Emperor Qin's terracotta pits were built

These weapons are quite advanced masterpieces. They seemed to be more regular and sharp after being cast, rasped, drilled and polished. For example, the body of the bronze sword was gradually adapted to slice, while its thickness does the opposite. The curvature between the two sides of the sword is completely symmetrical, as in accordance with the mechanical theory. It is really a miracle that the weapons were made so elaborate without modern tools.

Except exquisite technical skill, proportionate alloy components are thoroughly scientific. As we all know, for bronze products, different ratios of metallic elements will decide its rigidity, toughness, and other mechanical performances. An ancient Chinese science book, named 'Kao Gongji', especially recorded six kinds of optimal ratios between copper and tin, and these data were called 'Liu Qi'. Through testing, the sword and spear, the ratio between copper and tin is

Bronze crossbow

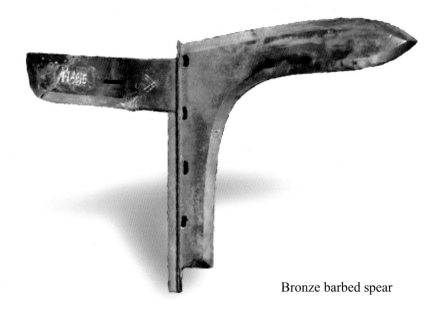

Bronze barbed spear

Bronze Shu (weapon)

Bronze dagger

close to the ratio that is recorded in 'Kao Gongji'. However, the bronze arrows contain more lead, and less tin. Because lead is poisonous, the arrows are even more deadly. All of these indicated that the people of Emperor Qin had surmised a compara-tively scientific criteria for ratios amongst different metal elements.

Especially, the unearthed weapons from the pits demonstrate that temporal people have acquired wonderful accomplishments in the side of antirust technology. Many bronze weapons, through buried under-ground for over 2,200 years, still glitter in metallic luster. Scientific and technical examination reveals that these weapons are coated with a thin layer of oxidized chromium whilst being made. But not until modern times, did European countries and the United States master this kind of technology. It is not just a miracle in the history of metallurgical industry.

As we all know, the quality of weapon equipment is very important in battle effectiveness. Emperor Qin's conquest of the other six rival states and unification of the whole China was due to excellent weapon equipment to a certain degree.

Splendid Treasure of House of Ancient Sculpture

The treasure house of ancient Chinese sculptures has a long history and excellent tradition. Away in the New-Stone Period, there existed some small colorful sculptural head portraits. Since Shang Dynasty and Zhou Dynasty, arts of sculpture obtained some development; while in the Qin Dynasty, it experienced audaciously innovation. Throwing off flashy and petty peculiarity from former dynasty, arts of sculpture in Qin Dynasty made a great progress. At the same time, differences from those introduced from foreign countries, sculp-

Terracotta warrior in amour

Terracotta warrior in amour

Terracotta Warrior in battle tunics

Terracotta charioteer

ture in Qin Dynasty embodied the original aggressive spirit. The pits of the terracotta armoured warriors and horses form an ancient treasure house imbued not only with rich military concepts, but also with splendid sculptural arts.

Achievements of terracotta sculptural arts are as follows. In the first place, it is rich in large numbers, tall figure and sublime scenery. Nearly 8,000 life-size sculptures of the terracotta armoured warriors and horses are arrayed in imitation of the Qin battle formation in the three

Terracotta charioteer▶

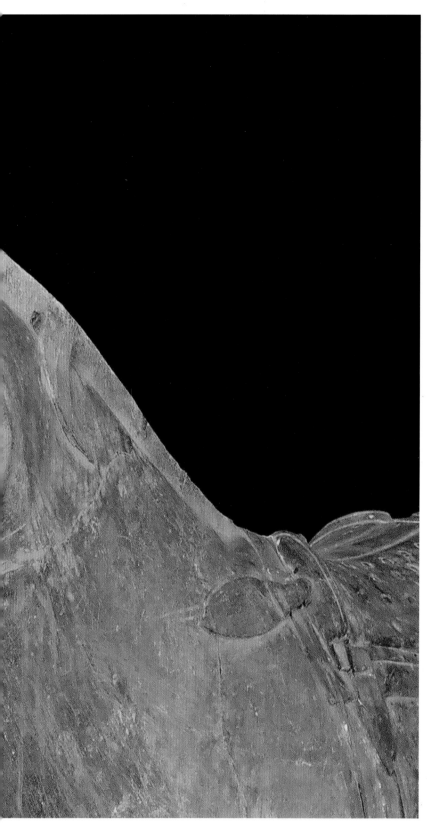

Terracotta Horse head

pits totaling more than 20,000 square meters. The terracotta armoured warriors and horses are 1.8 to 2 meters tall. The grandiose layout of so large an army has such tremendous momentum it presents a striking artistic appeal of conquest and invincibility.

Secondly, simplicity and accuracy is the other art feature of them, which could be concluded through more than a thousand excavated Terracotta figures. These prototype art pieces followed the realistic disciplines and accurate proportions, which seems every single one is a duplicate of its own real model. Generally, the Terracotta horses possess an attacking gesture and strong spirit; whilst the different types of Terracotta figures according to the military level, for instance generals, commander officials and warriors, have various gestures and personalities.

Terracotta generals normally are a good height, covered in splendored and colourful armours and hats. Commander officials are more in jerkins and tall hats, armed with weapons.

Terracotta general

Back view of the
terracotta general

As to the warriors, which are categorised into standing archers, kneeling archers, Infantry and Cavalry according to different tasks. What we can still notice is the archers' fighting poses but the weapons are invisible which were eroded.

Terracotta archer

Kneeling archer in Pits 2▶

Painted terracotta warrior head   Terracotta general head

The good size and nice shape seems are not the most touching and attractive part of these Terracotta warriors, but the various and detailed expressions on their faces and hair styles. We could say that every single figure is a piece of fine art work, which is because of the subtle and detailed work on the figures' heads, hence no duplicate or twin brothers' face could be found. Some show an open mind character, some serious, some angry, some lost in their thinking and some smiling; every different facial expression gives you a peculiar story of its own. The attractiveness of its art value is so significant and unique, which would be as important as ancient Greek and Roman sculptural art.

Terracotta general head

Painted terracotta warrior head

Painted terracotta warrior head

Painted terracotta warrior head

Painted terracotta warrior head

Painted terracotta warrior head

Head of terracotta warrior in jerkin

Painted terracotta warrior head　　Painted terracotta warrior head　　Head of terracotta warrior in amour

Head of terracotta warrior in jerkin　　Head of terracotta warrior in amour　　Head of terracotta warrior in amour

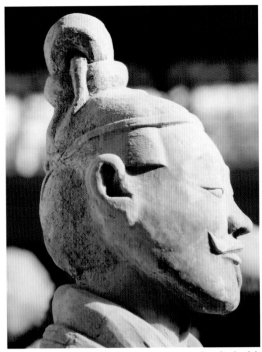

Head of terracotta warrior in jerkin

Head of terracotta warrior in jerkin

Head of terracotta warrior

Head of terracotta warrior

Terracotta horse

In the third place, its splendid colors were highly praised. Although the terracotta armoured warriors and horses survived the catastrophic conflagration and withstood underground moisture and soil erosion of over 2,000 tears, colors can still be spotted sticking to some of these figures. A dozen mineral dyes used included bright reds, pinks, powder greens, powder purples, sky blues, orange-yellows, whites and umber, mostly being reds, green, blue and umber. The sharp contrast between the warm colors and the cool ones that were painted on them set the keynotes of liveliness and magnificence. It is calculated that there are almost over 8,000 terracotta armoured warriors and horses. Supposing that each one is 1.75 square meters, the whole project would be a huge frame with 12 kilometers long and 1 meter wide. Just imagine what gorgeous colors such a huge army possessed. This, on one hand, reflects the aesthetic views of the Qin

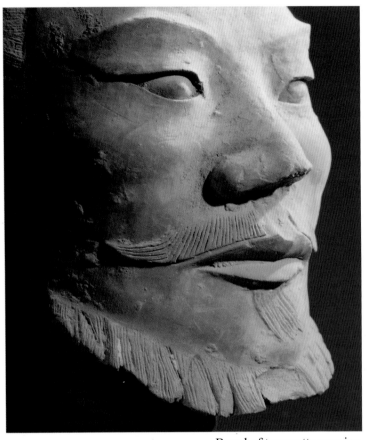

Beard of terracotta warrior

people, and on the other hand, deliberately or unintentionally weakens the innate atmosphere of solemness and horror in works of arts on military themes, thus bringing about thrilling scenes of abounding vitality , high morale and all-conquering bravery.

Moreover, a number of crafts were applied in pottery-making, with moulding as the mainstay to be supplemented by heating-up , and-shaing, carving and painting. As described above, it is really a complicated process in potterymaking, how could all these be finished since most workers were amateurish? The modeling of the pottery warriors and horses was vivid and precise. They were baked in kilns under an accurate control of contraction tolerance at the temperatures approximately between 950 degree and 1,050 degree. The finished pottery figures looked all the more elegant with pure luster, high density and great solidity, and gave out clanging sounds when knocked. The same principles of construction were employed in the making of the horses. The legs of the horses were all solid pottery to ensure that they would be strong. The head, body and tail were all molded or modeled separately and then fixed to the legs. The various details of the eyes, nostrils and mouth of the horses were sculpted the same way as the human figures. This shows that China's pottery-making craftsmanship already reached the consummate level 2,200 years ago.

In a word, the terracotta armoured warriors and horses combine unitary style with the beauty of individuality, appearing like a bright pearl in the history of ancient Chinese sculpture. The beauty of terracotta armoured warriors and horses is full of invigoration, solemness and

Close-up view of warrior's eye

Beard of terracotta warrior

Hat of terracotta general

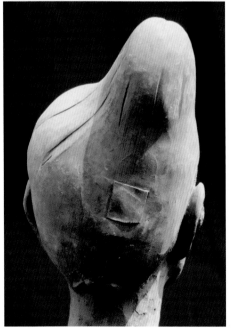

Hat of terracotta warrior

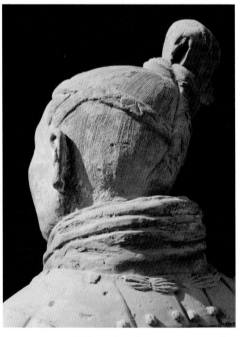

Hair style of terracotta warrior

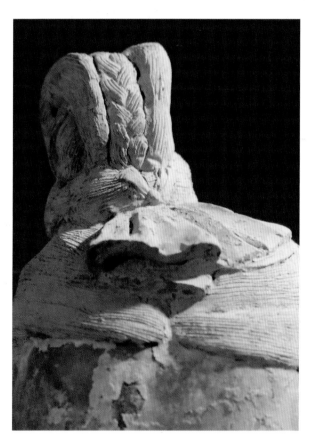

Hair style of terracotta warrior

Hair style of terracotta warrior

Belt

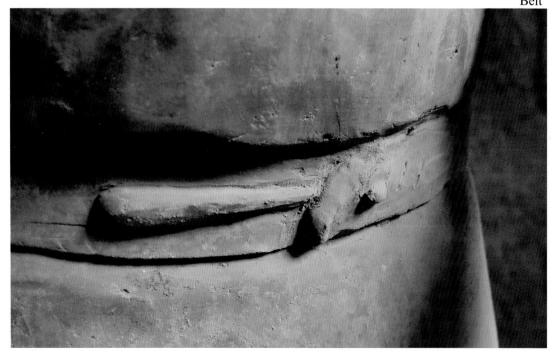

Belt

Belt

Belt

Close-up view of warrior's hand

Close-up view of warrior's hand

Close-up view of warrior's hand

Close-up view of warrior's foot

Close-up view of warrior's foot

Close-up view of warrior's foot

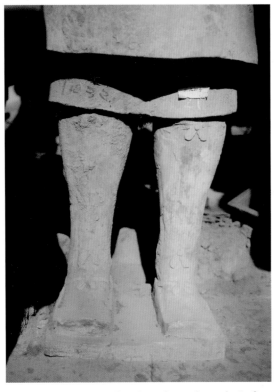

Close-up view of warrior's foot

Sole of archer's shoes

Warrior's amour

inspiration, through which the character of Qin Dynasty was thoroughly showed. Imagine that thousands upon thousands of soldiers are all preparing for the war with swords in their arms. Also imagine that those soldiers are trying their best to vanquish their enemies. The beauty of terracotta armoured warriors and horses, without question, is deep and spiritual. Compared with the former and later sculptures such as a grotto, temple, mausoleum and other underground sculptures, the sculpture of Emperor Qin's Terracotta Museum seem to be better.

In ancient feudal society, the status of those craftsmen was quite low-down, neither their stories nor their names could be found. Fortunately, to strengthen the management of those workers, the system of marking their names was pushed. In this way, we can probably confirm their names.

In fact, those who worked on the terracotta armoured warriors and horses were a group of potters. Some of them came from the ceramics factories in the court but not others, but all of them were seasoned craftsmen. On the careful research of all the terracotta armoured warriors and horses, the name of over 80 craftsmen have been so far discovered. All those craftsmen came from all over the country. Because of their different experiences and sufferings, and because of their different teachers, great diversity could be found. Generally speaking, sculptures of the craftsmen from the court showed more precise and innovative while those from plebeian have form and colorful. Despite these differences, all of them were real creator of terra-cotta sculptural arts. They developed themselves to the whole of terracotta sculpture.

Warrior's amour

Bronze Chariots and Horses
——Acme of Bronzes

In Emperor Qin's terracotta museum, you can imagine grandiose lineup through the Pits 1, 2 and 3. Furthermore, also, you can enjoy the beauty of ancient bronze arts by Emperor Qin's bronze carriage and horses.

Excavated site of bronze carriage and horses

According to the records, there were five times Emperor Qin inspected all over the country. In each time, his motorcades were immensely imposing. People may wonder that what on earth were Emperor Qin's chariots and horses? It was nothing but the unearthed Chariots and horses which gave us an answer. In December 1980, the bronze chariots and horses were excavated in an attendant burial pit 20 meters west to the mound of Qin Shi Huang Mausoleum.

Bronze charioteer of
'No.1 bronze carriage'

Back view of 'No. 1 bro
carriage bronze chariote

No. 1 bronze carriage and horses

Part of No. 1 bronze carriage and horses▶

No. 2 bronze carriage and horses

The chariots and horses are the biggest and most realistic chariots and horses that have been unearthed so far. Investigation reveals that the chariots and horses were the deluxe sedans to be used to by the Emperor when he went on inspection tours in his after-life. They were modeled after the real chariot, horse and driver, but were half the size. According to the order of the two chariots and horses be unearthed, those two sets were named No. 1 Bronze Chariot and Horses (the front chariot) and No. 2 Bronze Chariot and Horses (the back chariot). The two sets, almost half the actual size, were found facing west, one preceding the other, in a big wooden coffin about 7 meters long and 2.3 meters wide. Both of the two bronze chariots had a single shaft and two wheels, in front of which were four horses with were approximately 90 centimeters high, 110 centimeters long and 170-200 kilograms weight. The four horses, lining abreast, are painted white all over. The No.1 chariot, also named with "the Higher Chariot" and "the Standing Chariot", was to lead the fleet of imperial chariots and horses when Qin Shi Huang went on a tour of inspection. The carriage is a rectangular

No. 2 bronze carriage

shape, 1.26 meters wide and 0.70 meters long, topped with a round bronze umbrella of 1.22 meters in diameter, under which stands a bronze charioteer, with a long sword at the waist. On the outer side of the left protecting board is a quiver in which 12 bronze arrows are laid. On the inner side of the right protecting board there is a bronze shield, with the height of 36.2 centimeters, inserted in a set of silver shield-holders. Both sides of the shield are colorfully painted with cloud-like patterns. This shield is the most complete shield ever discovered from the Qin Dynasty. Four horses, fleshy and muscular, stand with heads raised as if they are ready to gallop at a whip from the charioteer. The No. 2 chariot, called the chariot with seats or the chariot with beds, has a total length of 3.17 meters and a height of 1.06 meters, weighing 1,241 kilograms. The convex-shaped carriage comprises two compartments. The front compartment is for the charioteer, and the back one, for the Emperor. The bronze charioteer in the front compartment, wearing a long robe and a doubled-tailed hat, sits on his knees to a height of 0.51 meters, a short sword at the waist and his hands stretched out holding reins. With a smiling

Bronze charioteer of
No. 2 bronze carriage

Silver and gold gilded canopy pole ▶

Horse head-piece

face and focused mind, the charioteer looks care-free, content and cautious to be a fine bronze sculpture of rare value. The back chamber is quite spacious, the window panels of which are cast into shallow diamond-flower holes, which are neatly aligned into rhombic patterns. The holes are used for ventilation. Therefore, the No. 2 Chariot is also called "Air-conditioned Chariot". The roof of the carriage is a turtle-shell canopy, which reflects the ancient thoughts of old China.

As is known to all, the arts of bronze sculpture of our country reached its zenith in the times of Shang Dynasty and Zhou Dynasty, which are also called the times of bronze. With the appearance and increase of ironware, it gradually decreased. There were almost no bronze sculptures could be seen in the Qin Dynasty, not to mention Han Dynasty. The discovery about the chariots and horses changed what we knew. To a certain degree, the chariots and horses combined the best skills in that dynasty and provided us a new look to the Qin Dynasty. The technological process in making the bronze chariots and horses also attained an increasingly high lever. The No. 1 chariots and horses alone has 3,064 components while the No. 2 has 3,462, of which over 1,000 odd are silver and gold pieces. The whole process involves casting, welding, sticking, chiseling, carving, polishing, and inlaying, out of which quite a few are inventions by craftsmen of the Qin Dynasty. Both chariots were originally painted with bright colors ranging from vermilion, pink, green, blue to white but the basic color was white. There are more than ten

chariot wheel

Winch of the horse

color patterns on the chariots depicting dragons, phoenixes, clouds and geometric designs. We can imagine that what a luxurious life Emperor Qin lived through the chariots and horses.

The two sets, founded in an attendant burial pit 20 meters west to the mound of Qin Shi Huang Mausoleum, in a big wooden coffin about 7 meters long and 2.3 meters wide. Due to the wood having rotted and the earthen layers collapsing, the chariots and horses were found unearthed in thousands of pieces. Fortunately, the pieces were scattered on the ground. After several years of painstaking restoration, two complete sets of bronze chariots and horses are on display in the museum. The chariots and horses are well rated as "the crown of the bronzes". It is rare in the archeological world to discover both in China from all over the world. The discovery of the bronze chariots and horses makes the grand occasions of the imperial procession of Qin Shi Huang seen through the real objects and provides precious substantial materials to know and study the ancient imperial chariot institution. It also fully reflects China's superb technological level in metalworking over 2,000 years ago and fine wisdom and great talents of the ancient Chinese laboring people.

Horse Bit

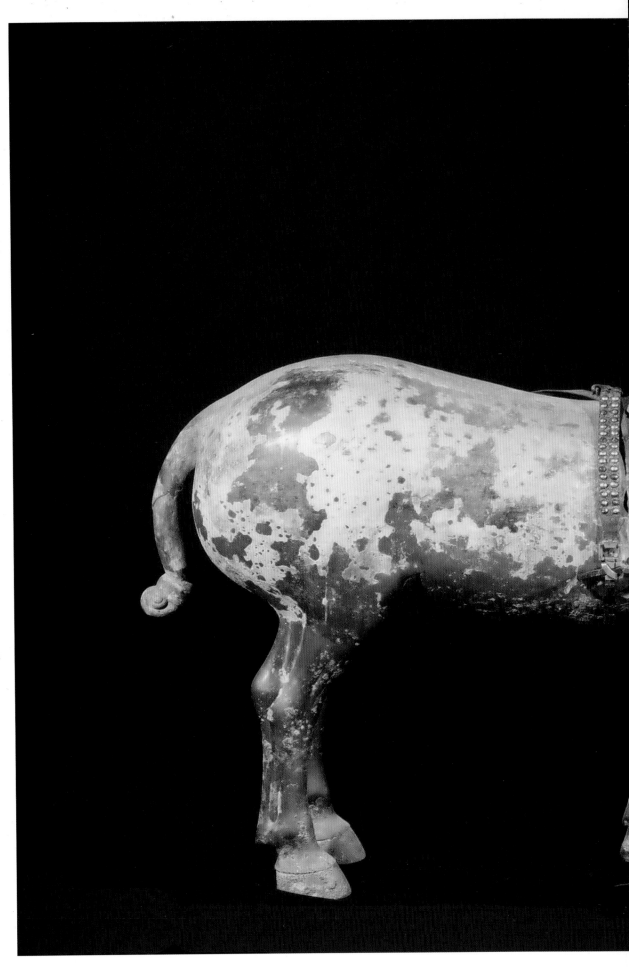

Bronze horse on right

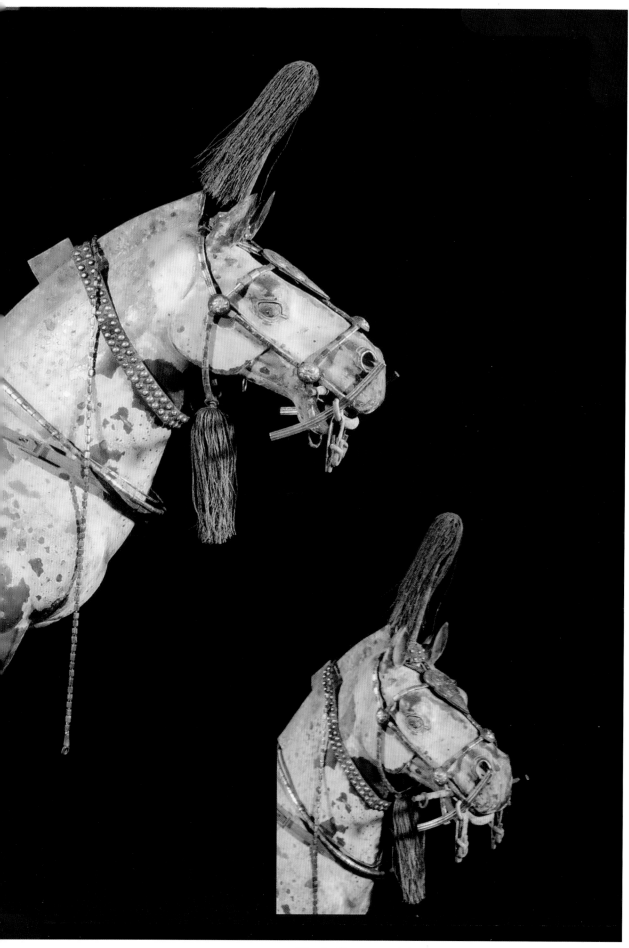

Head of horse on right

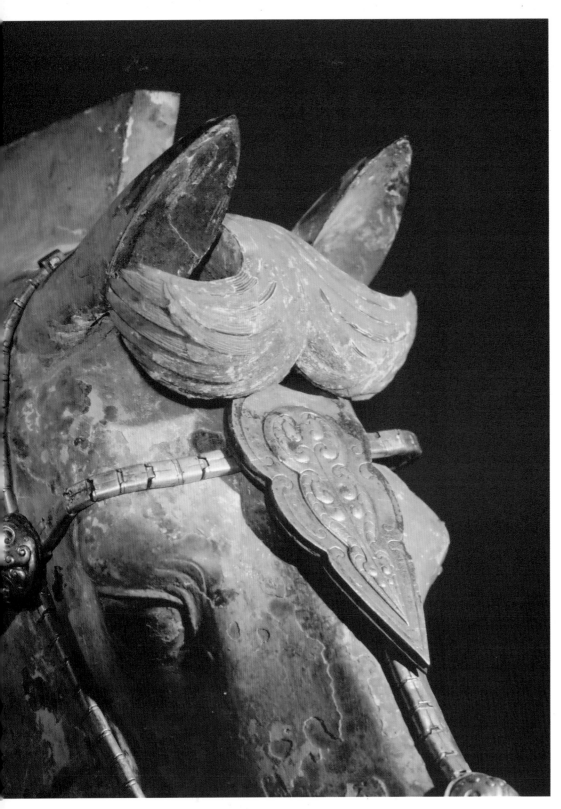

Ornament of terracotta horse

Head of 'No. 2 bronze carriage' horse▶

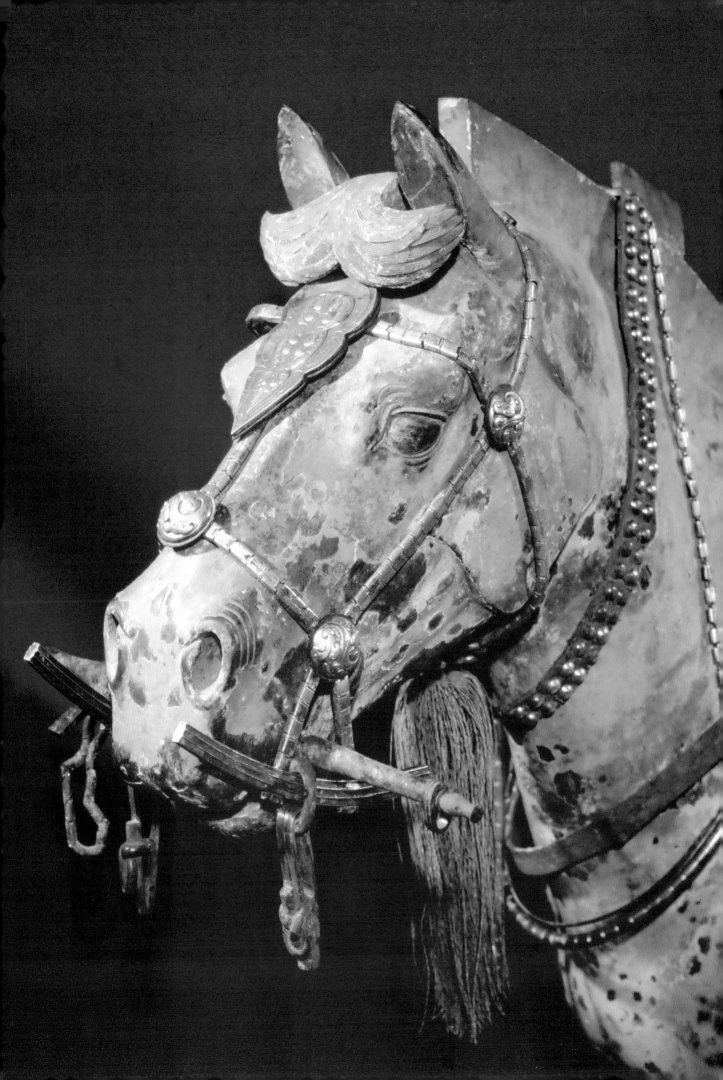

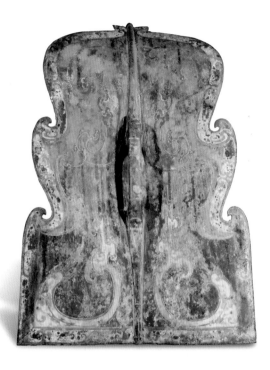

Bronze square-pot

Painted bronze shield

Bow rest

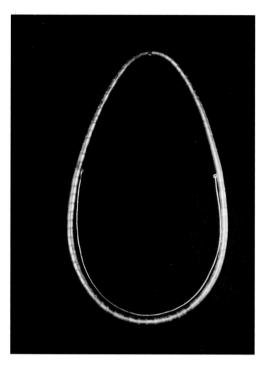

Silver Choker

Designs of painted door

Designs of painted window